Lower Fields Primary School

MOUNTAINS

BY
MIKE CLARK

©2017
Book Life
King's Lynn
Norfolk PE30 4LS

Written by:
Mike Clark

Edited by:
Charlie Ogden

Designed by:
Drue Rintoul

ISBN: 978-1-78637-184-3

All rights reserved
Printed in Malaysia

A catalogue record for this book is available from the British Library.

Photocredits

Abbreviations: l-left, r-right, b-bottom, t-top, c-centre, m-middle.

Front Cover Main – Galyna Andrushko. FCR – azure1. 1 – Iakov Filimonov. 2 – Ruslan Gusev. 4tr – Tatiana Belova. 4b – South12th Photography. 5 – Ann Cantelow. 7 – Daniel Prudek. 8t – Nina B. 8b – Victor Lauer. 9tr – Vixit. 9c – aleksandr hunta. 9b – Pichugin Dmitry. 10tr – Susan Flashman. 10b – Mary Ann McDonald. 11t – Mike Flippo. 11bl – By Thesurvived99 (Own work) [CC BY-SA 3.0 (http://creativecommons.org/licenses/by-sa/3.0)], via Wikimedia Commons. 12t – Soili Jussila. 12b – Peter Wey. 13 – Erni. 14tr – GGRIGOROV. 14b – elnavegante. 15 – BlueOrange Studio. 16tr – Belen Bilgic Schneider. 16b – Stephane Bidouze. 17tl – Henrik Larsson. 17b – Zety Akhzar. 18bl – Suha Derbent. 18r – Erick Margarita Images. 19tl – Johnny Adolphson. 19b – Krasowit. 20b – Mr.Ruj_Thailand. 20r – NancyS. 21tl – Graham R Prentice. 21r – Butterfly Hunter. 22tr – Iakov Filimonov. 22b – Ronnie Howard. 23t – Scott E Read. 23b – Alexandr Junek Imaging s.r.o.. 24tl – By Jamling Tenzing Norgay (http://www.tenzing-norgay-trekking.de) [GFDL (http://www.gnu.org/copyleft/fdl.html) or CC BY-SA 3.0 (http://creativecommons.org/licenses/by-sa/3.0)], via Wikimedia Commons. 24c – ixpert. 25tl – phugunfire. 25m – Suha Derbent. 25b – Dchauy. 26l – By Ali Zifan (Enhanced, modified, and vectorized). (Derived from World Koppen Classification.svg.) [CC BY-SA 4.0 (http://creativecommons.org/licenses/by-sa/4.0)], via Wikimedia Commons. 26b – POZZO DI BORGO Thomas. 26c – ixpert. 27t – AppStock. 27b – Dudarev Mikhail. 28bl – wrangler. 29br – Jacek Chabraszewski. Images are courtesy of Shutterstock.com. With thanks to Getty Images, Thinkstock Photo and iStockphoto.

CONTENTS

Page 4	Habitats and Biomes
Page 6	What Is a Mountain?
Page 8	Mountain Habitats
Page 10	At the Bottom
Page 12	Snowy Forests
Page 14	Mountain Tops
Page 16	Crawling Critters
Page 18	Rock Climbers
Page 20	Deep Sleepers
Page 22	Big Hunters
Page 24	Himalayas
Page 26	Madagascan Mountains
Page 28	Saving the Mountains
Page 30	Quick Quiz and Useful Links
Page 31	Glossary
Page 32	Index

Words in **bold** are explained in the glossary on page 31.

Habitats and Biomes

WHAT ARE HABITATS?

Habitats are places where plants and animals live. Habitats can include everything from mountains and rivers to deserts and oceans – even other living things!

The animals and plants that live in a habitat usually become **adapted** to it. This means that they become very good at raising their young and finding food and water in their specific habitat. A habitat can also keep the animal safe from **predators**, often by having lots of places to hide. This helps animals to **reproduce** safely.

A stork makes its nest high up in a tree. Up here, it is safe from predators that cannot fly or climb up the thin branches of the tree.

Animals and plants that only live on other living things are called parasites. A wood tick is a type of parasite that bites into an animal's skin and drinks its blood!

4

WHAT IS A BIOME?

A biome is a very large area of the world where the **climate** is very similar. Because biomes are so huge, they usually contain many different habitats. As a biome's climate is the same all the way across it, many of the animals and plants that live in the same biome will adapt similar **traits**, even if they live in very different habitats. While some animals and plants are able to live in different habitats within the same biome, most living things can only live in one habitat.

For example, the quaking aspen grows very tall and fast in places that receive lots of rain and sunlight. This is because it has big leaves that can absorb lots of sunlight to make food. However, in hot areas where there is very little rain, such as deserts, the aspen tree cannot **survive**.

*Some plants survive better in the dry, sunny conditions in the desert, whereas other plants survive better in the dark, damp conditions in the rainforest. This shows how living things adapt to their **environment**.*

What Is a Mountain?

A mountain is a natural rise in the Earth's surface that rises high above the surrounding area. For something to be called a mountain, it usually has to be over 600 metres tall.

Mountains are usually measured from the sea level to their peak. The peak of a mountain is its highest point. 'Sea level' is the height of the sea's surface. Because the sea is very flat, using the sea level as the starting point to measure mountains means that all mountains are measured from the same place.

Mountains are found all around the world. Mountains are created by the movement of **tectonic plates**. Most mountains are found in mountain ranges, which are huge areas of land that are covered by many mountains.

800 metres

Atlas Mountains
Location: Africa
Length: 2,500 km

Rockies
Location: North America
Length: 4,800 km

Andes
Location: South America
Length: 7,000 km

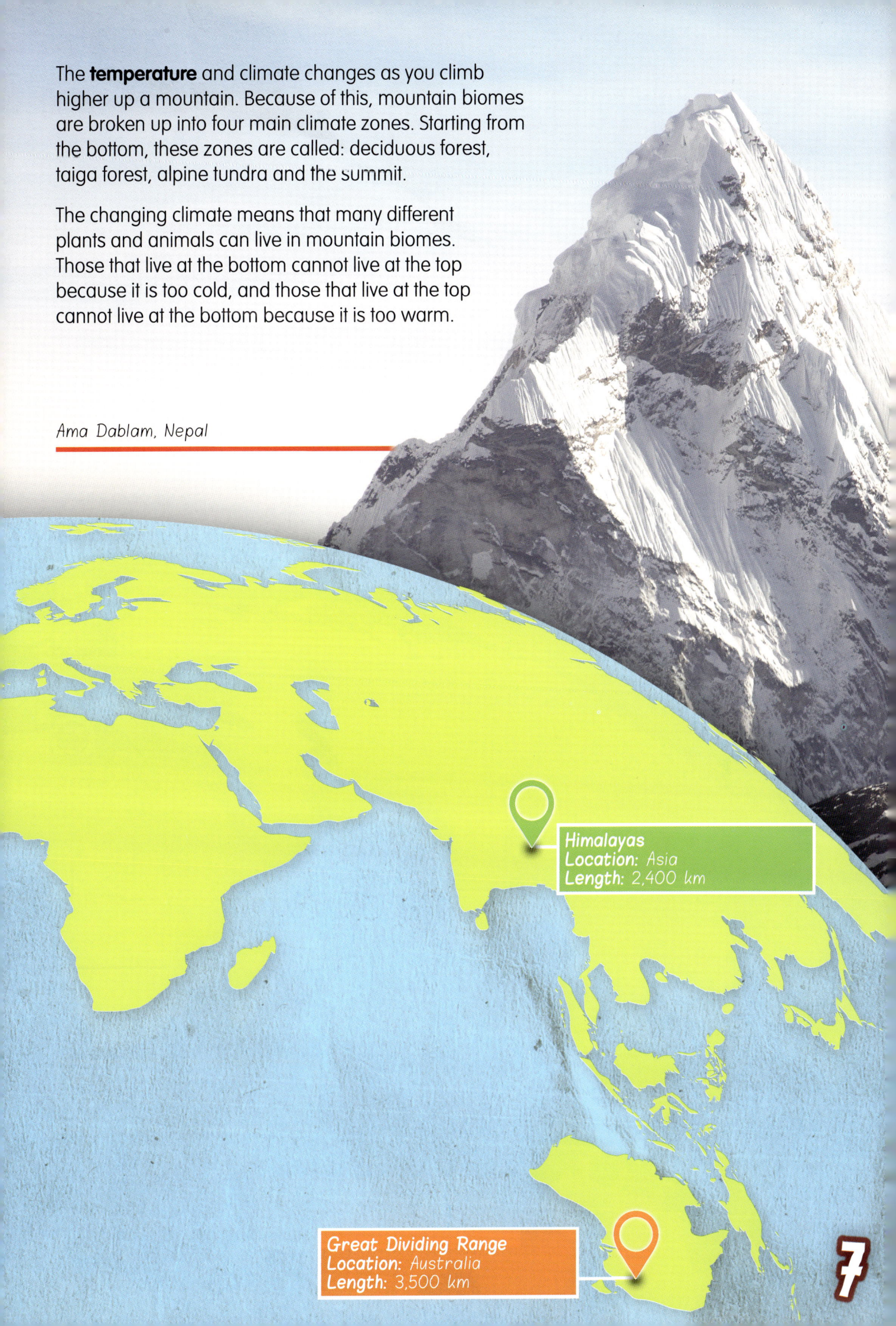

The **temperature** and climate changes as you climb higher up a mountain. Because of this, mountain biomes are broken up into four main climate zones. Starting from the bottom, these zones are called: deciduous forest, taiga forest, alpine tundra and the summit.

The changing climate means that many different plants and animals can live in mountain biomes. Those that live at the bottom cannot live at the top because it is too cold, and those that live at the top cannot live at the bottom because it is too warm.

Ama Dablam, Nepal

Himalayas
Location: Asia
Length: 2,400 km

Great Dividing Range
Location: Australia
Length: 3,500 km

Mountain Habitats

Because mountain biomes have a variety of climates, they contain many different habitats that are home to a range of different animals.

At the Bottom

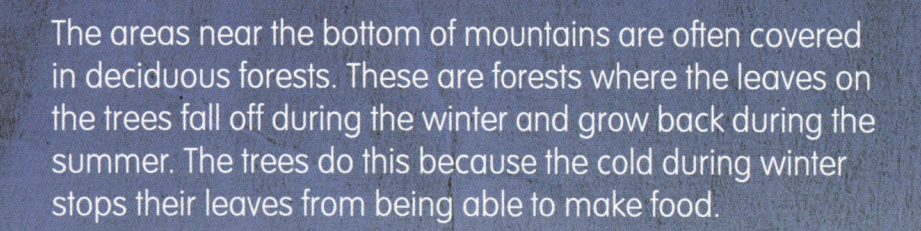

The areas near the bottom of mountains are often covered in deciduous forests. These are forests where the leaves on the trees fall off during the winter and grow back during the summer. The trees do this because the cold during winter stops their leaves from being able to make food.

The word deciduous means 'to fall down'. This refers to how the leaves fall off the trees.

Sangre de Cristo Mountains, Colorado

Snow Forest

Snow Forests

Above the deciduous forests are taigas, which are also known as snow forests. The leaves of the trees in snow forests do not fall off during the winter. Instead, their small, thick leaves are covered in a special waxy coating that protects them from the cold. This causes the trees to grow slower, but means that they can absorb sunlight all year round.

Tundras & Mountain Tops

Above the snow forests are alpine tundras. Tundras are areas where no trees can grow because the climate is too cold. If something is 'alpine' it means that it is to do with mountains. Above the alpine tundras are the mountain tops, which are called summits. The summits of mountains are often covered in snow.

The temperature at the summit of Mount Everest can be as low as −36 °C.

Alpine Tundra

Not all mountains have all four zones – a deciduous forest, a snow forest, an alpine tundra and a snowy summit. This is because some mountains are not as tall as others, meaning that they don't have cold summits. As well as this, some mountains sit near to or on the Equator, meaning that they have a warm climate at all levels. Others sit very close to the North Pole or South Pole and therefore have a cold climate all over.

The Hoggar Mountains in the Sahara have a very hot climate all the way up because they are near the Equator.

At the Bottom

Deciduous forests are found all around the world. They are normally found on the lower slopes of mountains where the temperature is neither too high nor too low.

The tree kangaroo lives in deciduous forests on the slopes of mountains in northern Australia and Papua New Guinea. They have adapted to have large, padded feet that help to give them extra grip. They also have a long tail that helps them to balance. These adaptations help them to hold onto the branches of trees.

The deciduous forests near the bottom of mountains can still get very cold during the winter. Because of this, many animals have had to adapt so that they can remain in their habitat all year round. Mountain gorillas have thick fur and short limbs, which helps them to stay warm even in the winter.

Tree Kangaroo

Mountain gorillas living in the Virunga Mountains in East Africa.

Giant pandas live in deciduous forests on the slopes of mountains in China. They spend most of their day eating lots of bamboo, which is a type of grass. Giant pandas are very bad at **digesting** bamboo, meaning that eating it gives them very little energy. This makes them one of the most confusing animals and scientists still don't know why giant pandas choose to eat bamboo.

Giant pandas eat the bamboo that gives them the most energy. This changes during the seasons. During the summer, the bamboo higher the up the mountain gives the pandas more energy. During the winter, bamboo lower down the mountain gives the pandas more energy. Giant pandas move up and down the mountains they live on in order to find the bamboo that will provide them with the most energy.

Arrow bamboo is a type of bamboo. It is called this because Japanese warriors, known as samurai, used to use the bamboo to make arrows a long time ago.

Snowy Forests

Snow forests are much colder than deciduous forests and are filled with trees that have small, tough leaves. These trees are known as evergreens.

The wolverine is a predator that lives in the snow forests of North America. Its thick coat keeps it warm during the winter, when the forest becomes covered in snow. The wolverine can also spread out its toes, making its feet twice as big as normal. Doing this helps the wolverine to walk on top of the snow.

During winter, snow forests are completely covered in snow. This makes it hard for many animals to hide from predators. This is because they are covered in dark fur that makes it easy for predators to spot them against the white snow. Because of this, the mountain hare changes colour and grows white fur during the winter, which helps it to blend in with the snow.

Can you see the mountain hare?

12

The great grey owl can be found flying around in the mountains of North America. This bird mostly hunts during the night when it is hard to see. In order to help it find its prey, the great grey owl has adapted feathers that grow around its face like a disc. This large disc pushes sound towards the owl's ears. This helps the owl to hear its prey from very far away.

Great Grey Owl

The owl's hearing is so good that it can hear an animal that is under 60 cm of snow.

Mountain Tops

The climate high up in mountains is often extremely cold. Animals that live on mountain tops have adapted to be able to stay warm in their habitat.

Many animals, such as wild yaks, grow an extremely thick coat of fur to survive the cold. Wild yaks are large animals that live high in the mountains of Tibet, where the temperature often drops below 0 °C. The wild yak's fur coat is so long that it hangs over its chest and protects its legs from the freezing cold winds.

The air at the top of very high mountains often has very little **oxygen** in it. Because of this, the air is said to be 'thin'. In order to deal with this, the guanaco llama, which lives on mountains in Chile, has more **red blood cells** in its blood than most animals. This is because red blood cells absorb oxygen, meaning that the more red blood cells an animal has, the faster it can take oxygen into its body.

Wild Yak

Guanaco llamas have about four times more red blood cells than humans.

Japanese Macaques

Most monkeys live in very warm climates, but not all do. A group of Japanese macaques, which are also called snow monkeys, live at the tops of snowy mountains in Japan. They keep warm by bathing in hot pools of water, called onsens, that can be found on the slopes of the mountains. 'Onsen' is the Japanese name for a hot spring. These hot springs form when water gets trapped underground and is warmed by the heat of the Earth, before being pushed to the surface.

These Japanese macaques are keeping warm in a mountain onsen.

The Japanese macaques can survive temperatures as cold as −15 °C.

Crawling Critters

Most mountain habitats are full of critters of every shape and size, many of which have special adaptations that allow them to survive in different mountain climates and habitats.

Many caterpillars are the same colour as the leaves they eat because this helps them to avoid being seen by predators. However, the spotted tussock moth caterpillar, which lives near the bottom of mountains in North America, is very easy to see. Its bright colours warn predators that it is **toxic** and that they should avoid eating it.

Stick insects can hide themselves in forests better than almost any other animal. Their bodies have adapted to look like a stick, making it very hard to find them in forests. They are mostly found in the deciduous forests that lie at the bottom of mountains in Asia and Australia.

Spotted Tussock Moth Caterpillar

A stick insect in a jungle in Malaysia.

Bark Beetle

The mountains in North America can get very cold. To protect its eggs from the cold, the bark beetle burrows into the bark of a tree and lays its eggs inside. Here they are safe from predators and the cold, winter weather.

The Himalayan jumping spider lives up to 6,700 metres high in the Himalayan mountains. Very few other animals can live this high up a mountain. There is very little food up at this level, so the spider survives by eating insects that get blown up to the top of the mountain by the wind.

The jumping spider has large eyes, making it good at spotting very small prey.

The jumping spider can jump a distance 50 times the length of its own body.

Rock Climbers

Mountains are often very rocky and steep. For animals that live on mountains like this, being a good climber is the difference between life and death.

One of the best climbers in mountain biomes is the alpine ibex. Alpine ibex live high in the mountains of northern Italy. They have specially-adapted **hooves** that are perfect for climbing. The hooves have sharp edges on the bottom that make it easier to grip the rocks.

One of the best predators in mountain biomes is the mountain lion. The mountain lion is the second largest cat in America. It is amazing at jumping and can leap up to four and a half metres into the air. This makes it excellent at surprising its prey.

Mountain Lion

Mountain lions are also known as pumas, cougars, panthers and catamounts.

The horns of an alpine ibex can grow up to one and a half metres long.

One fish that is very good at climbing is the salmon. Every year, huge groups of salmon swim upstream to return to the place where they hatched. Once they make it, they lay their own eggs. Most rivers start high up in mountains and flow downhill. Because of this, swimming upstream includes a lot of climbing and swimming against river **currents**.

The salmon go through all this effort so that they can make sure that their eggs have the best chance of survival. Up in the mountains, the eggs will be safe from other fish that might want to eat them. But getting up the mountain comes at a big cost. The trip is so tiring that the salmon die after they release their eggs.

Kokanee Salmon

Salmon can jump about three and a half metres into the air, which helps them to get up and over waterfalls.

Salmon often climb over 2,000 metres in order to lay their eggs.

Deep Sleepers

*In cold climates, many animals go into a long, deep sleep during the winter known as **hibernation**. This helps the animal to survive the winter without needing to look for food.*

Many animals cannot travel to a warmer climate during the winter. Instead, these animals have to stay in their habitat and survive the cold of the winter, which is why many choose to hibernate. When animals hibernate, they go into a deep sleep and their body uses little energy, meaning that they don't need to eat any food.

An Arctic ground squirrel hibernates underground for up to eight months at a time. During this time, it **burrows** into the ground and lets its body temperature drop to as low as -3 °C. Many of its **organs** work much more slowly or even shut down completely. No other land **mammal** can endure temperatures this low and survive.

Arctic Ground Squirrel

An Arctic ground squirrel peering out of its burrow.

Weta, New Zealand

The mountain stone weta, which lives in New Zealand, hibernates in the snow. Rather than dig a burrow into the ground to keep warm, the mountain stone weta simply allows itself to become frozen. It will then **thaw** during the summer and be completely unharmed.

Strangely, monarch butterflies hibernate only after they've travelled to a warmer climate. During their journey, they travel about 4,500 kilometres across North America, from the Rocky Mountains down to the mountain forests in central Mexico. When they arrive in the mountain forests, they come together in large groups, known as clusters, to hibernate. When they wake up, they fly back north for the summer.

Monarch Butterfly

Big Hunters

Apex predators are rarely hunted by any other animals. They are often the largest animal in their **food chain**.

The golden eagle is the largest bird to inhabit many mountains in Russia and Asia. It can have a **wingspan** of up to two and a half metres. The golden eagle only stays in the mountains during the summer, hunting small animals. This bird has very good eye-sight and can see prey up to three kilometres away.

The golden eagle has very powerful talons. A talon is a claw belonging to a bird of prey.

A grey wolf howling.

The northern Rocky Mountain wolf is a type of grey wolf that lives in North America. A Rocky Mountain wolf's fur changes colour as the seasons change, going from brown or black in the summer to light grey or white in the winter. They are one of the most successful predators in the world because they hunt in well-organised packs of about eight wolves each.

Wolves howl to warn other wolves to stay off their land. They also howl to help other wolves in their pack to find their way home.

Snow Leopard

Snow leopards mostly live in mountains in Asia. They live in icy cold alpine tundras, up to 4,500 metres above sea level. The snow leopard is a silent hunter – it can sneak around rocks and jump down onto its prey from a height of over one and a half metres.

One of the most impressive predators in the world is the brown bear. The brown bear has very sharp claws, a powerful bite and very thick fur for keeping warm. Brown bears are omnivores, meaning that they eat both meat and plants.

The brown bear is the largest animal in the world to hibernate.

The Himalayan brown bear lives in the Himalayan mountains.

Himalayas

The Himalayas is a mountain range in Asia. It is home to nine of the ten tallest mountains in the world, including the world's tallest mountain – Mount Everest – which stands at 8,848 metres tall.

The Himalayas cross through five countries: Bhutan, India, Nepal, China and Pakistan. Millions of years ago, India was an island separate from Asia. But, over millions of years, India slowly drifted towards Asia and eventually crashed into it. This crash caused the land to be pushed up, forming huge mountains.

The first people to climb all the way up to the top of Mount Everest were Edmund Hillary, from New Zealand, and Tenzing Norgay, from Nepal.

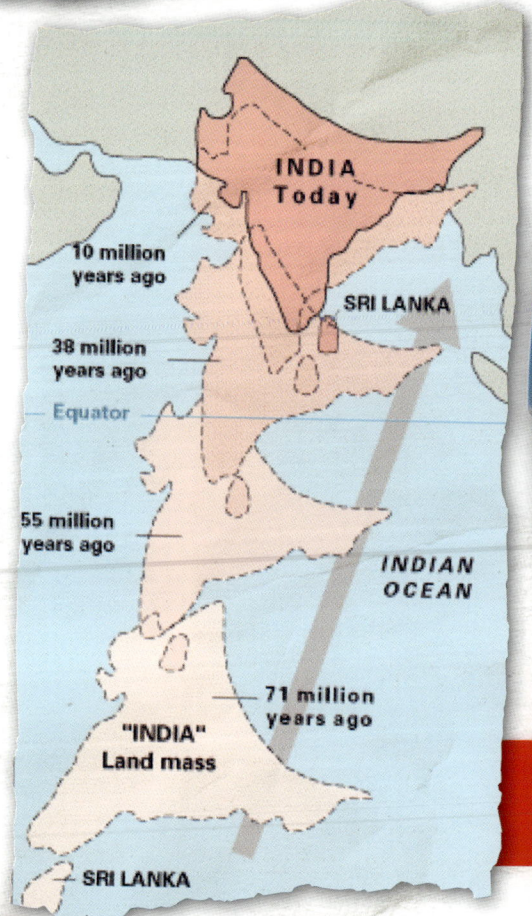

This is the path that India took before crashing into Asia and creating the Himalayan mountain range.

Jumping Spider

The mountains in the Himalayas have all four mountain climate zones. Because of this, many animals that live in the Himalayas have adapted to be able to live in a range of different habitats and climates - from freezing, rocky mountain tops to thick, deciduous forests.

Snow Leopard

The Himalayas are home to more species of animal than any other mountain range. Sadly, due to **deforestation**, many of these animals' habitats are being destroyed. This is making life for some animals very difficult and it could lead to certain species, such as the snow leopard, becoming **extinct**.

These forests at the base of the Himalayan mountains in India have been cut down to make room for farms.

25

Madagascan Mountains

The island of Madagascar is covered in lots of small mountains. The tallest of these is Maromokotro, which is only 2,876 metres high. These mountains are not high enough or cold enough to have snowy summits. What makes these mountains special is that they cause Madagascar to have many different climates.

The position of the island greatly affects its climate - one side faces the Indian Ocean, while the other side faces Africa. Cool winds from the Indian Ocean blow into Madagascar, causing cooler climates with lots of rain. However, the mountains block the cool ocean wind from moving all the way across the island. This means that the side of Madagascar facing Africa is much warmer and dryer.

Madagascan climates

- Tropical
- Temperate
- Desert

Africa

Madagascar has been an island for such a long time that many of the animals that live there do not live anywhere else in the world. One such animal is the lemur. This animal is a primate and looks a lot like a monkey, but it's actually classed as a lemuriform. These animals once had very small arms and legs, but over thousands of years the lemurs have adapted to have long arms and legs. These help the lemurs to climb trees and makes it easier for them to balance. This makes them almost as good at climbing as monkeys.

Ring-Tailed Lemur

The name 'lemur' means 'spirit of the night'.

Madagascar

Sadly, deforestation in Madagascar is happening very quickly and is making it difficult for the lemurs to survive. The bamboo lemur is now on a 'Red List' of endangered animals. This means that the bamboo lemur is at risk of becoming extinct if nothing is done about its loss of habitat.

Deforestation in Madagascar

Saving the Mountains

Global Warming

The greatest threat to the world's mountains is the Earth's rising temperature. As the temperature on Earth rises, alpine tundras shrink. This means that many animals that live in mountain habitats could find it hard to survive as their homes become too warm for them.

1990

2003

The amount of ice on the Sudiram mountain range in Papua Province, Indonesia, has greatly reduced in recent years.

Car exhausts release a lot of carbon dioxide into the atmosphere.

The planet is getting warmer due to gases, such as carbon dioxide, building up in the Earth's **atmosphere**. Carbon dioxide is always in the air, but it is a greenhouse gas which means too much of it stops the Sun's heat from escaping the Earth. Reducing the amount of carbon dioxide in the air is the best way to stop global warming.

One of the best ways to reduce the amount of carbon dioxide in the atmosphere is to grow plants. Plants absorb carbon dioxide and turn it into oxygen. By planting a tree or growing your own vegetables, you can help to reduce carbon dioxide levels and the effects of global warming.

Many vehicles, such as cars, give off a lot of carbon dioxide. The more we use them, the more carbon dioxide is released into the air, meaning that we should try to walk and cycle as much as we can. For long journeys, we should try to take the bus because when we share a journey with others, we reduce the number of vehicles on the road.

Quick Quiz and Useful Links

Quick Quiz

How tall must a hill be to be called a mountain?

What are the four main climate zones on a mountain called?

How have mountain gorillas adapted to survive in colder climates?

What is an onsen?

How high can a salmon jump?

How cold can an Arctic ground squirrel get during hibernation?

What is the largest mountain in the world?

What is the main cause of global warming?

Useful Links

Discover more about animals and their habitats by visiting
www.ngkids.co.uk

Find loads of mountainous wildlife videos and images at
www.bbc.co.uk/nature/habitats/mountain

Learn more about mountain habitats and animals under threat at
www.wwf.org.uk

Find out how you can help to stop global warming at
climatekids.nasa.gov/menu/big-questions

Glossary

°C	the symbol for degrees Celsius, the metric measurement of temperature
adapted	changed over time to suit different conditions
atmosphere	the mixture of gases that make up the air and surround the Earth
burrows	digs a hole or tunnel into the ground
climate	the common weather in a certain place
currents	steady flows of water in one direction
deforestation	the cutting down and removal of trees in a forest
extinct	a species of animal that is no longer alive
hibernation	sleeping for a very long time during winter to avoid the need to search for food
hooves	the horny parts of the feet of some animals, such as a horse
mammal	an animal that has warm blood, a backbone and produces milk
organs	parts of the body that have their own specific jobs or functions
oxygen	a natural gas that all living things need in order to survive
predators	animals that hunt other animals for food
red blood cells	tiny cells in blood that transport oxygen and carbon dioxide to and from the body
reproduce	have young through the act of mating
survive	continue to live
tectonic plates	the slabs of the Earth's crust that slowly drift around, changing the face of the planet
temperate	areas of the world where the weather is cold in winter and warm in summer
temperature	how hot something is
thaw	slowly become unfrozen as a result of warming up
toxic	able to cause injury or death when eaten or touched
tropical	hot and humid weather in areas near the Equator
wingspan	the distance the between the tips of a bird's wings

Index

A
adaptations 4–5, 10, 13–14, 16, 18, 25, 27, 30
Africa 6, 10, 26
air 14, 18–19, 23, 28–29
apex predators 22
Asia 7, 16, 22–24

B
bamboo 11, 27
bears 23
birds 13, 22
butterflies 21

C
climate 5, 7–9, 14–16, 20–21, 25–26, 30

D
deciduous forests 7–12, 16, 25
deforestation 25, 27

E
eggs 17, 19
extinct 25, 27

F
fish 19
flight 4, 13, 21
food 4–5, 8, 17, 20, 22

G
global warming 28–30
goats 18

H
hibernation 20–21, 23, 30
Himalayas 7, 24–25
hunting 13, 22–23

I
India 24–26
insects 16–17

J
jumping 17–19, 23, 25, 30

L
leaves 5, 8, 12, 16

M
Madagascar 26–27
monkeys 15, 27
mountain lion 18
mountain ranges 6, 24–25, 28
Mount Everest 9, 24

N
North America 6, 12–13, 16–17, 21–22

O
onsens 15, 30

P
pandas 11
Papua New Guinea 10
plants 4–5, 7, 23, 29
predators 4, 12, 16–18, 22–23
prey 13, 17–18, 22–23

R
rivers 4, 19

S
snow 8–9, 12–13, 15, 21, 23, 25–26
spiders 17, 25

T
temperature 7, 9–10, 14–15, 20, 28

Y
yaks 14